D1566006

SEDEM STUDIORUM

LOO

NIVERSITY

NATHAN JOYCE

DOG 'N' BONE

Published in 2019 by Dog 'n' Bone Books
An imprint of Ryland Peters & Small Ltd

20–21 Jockey's Fields   341 E 116th St
London   New York,
WC1R 4BW   NY 10029

www.rylandpeters.com

10 9 8 7 6 5 4 3 2 1

Text © Nathan Joyce 2019
Design © Dog 'n' Bone Books 2019

A CIP catalog record for this book is available
from the Library of Congress and the British
Library.

ISBN: 978 1 911026 83 9

Printed in China

Designer: Eoghan O'Brien
Editor: Dawn Bates

Thanks a lot to Eoghan for the cracking
design, to Dawn for the sterling editorial work,
and to Patricia for the repro. Thanks to Pete
and Cindy for their legacy of now associating
me with the word "toilet" forever. And lastly, a
special mention to my transatlantic brother
from another mother, Charlie Beckerman.

Contents

CHAPTER

1

LITERATURE

WAR AND PEACE

Written by Russian novelist **Leo Tolstoy** (1828–1910), and published in its entirety in **1869** (having previously been serialized), *War and Peace* observes the impact the **French invasion of Russia in 1812** had on several aristocratic families.

The novel opens with a society party in St Petersburg. Attending are **Pierre Bezukhov**, the clumsy but amiable illegitimate son of a rich dying count, and his friend, the charming **Prince Andrei Bolkonsky**, who has grown disenchanted with life. Andrei finds a military posting, leaving behind a wife, **Lise**, and sister, **Maria**. Meanwhile, in Moscow are the financially precarious **Rostov family** with their children, including **Nikolai**, who also joins the army, and the spirited **Natasha**.

Nikolai and Andrei fight in the **Battle of Austerlitz**, in which Andrei is wounded and captured. He meets **Napoleon Bonaparte** and becomes nihilistic. Meanwhile, **Count Bezukhov dies**, leaving **Pierre the wealthiest bachelor** in St Petersburg. He marries beautiful Princess **Hélène Kuragina**, who is **unfaithful**, so Pierre **challenges** her lover, **Dolokhov**, a skilled fighter, to a **duel**. Unexpectedly, Pierre wins, then leaves Hélène and becomes spiritually bereft, **seeking solace as a freemason**.

Andrei recovers and returns home to find **Lise dying in childbirth**. Although the child survives, Andrei is wracked with guilt. Hélène begs Pierre to **take her back**, which he does. **Andrei sees Natasha at a ball** in St Petersburg. **He falls in love with her** and **proposes marriage**. However, Andrei's father dislikes the Rostovs and insists the union is **delayed for a year**. Andrei travels abroad and Natasha is seduced by Hélène's brother, Anatole. Natasha **breaks off the engagement**. She plans to **elope** with Anatole, but Pierre tells her Anatole is **already married**. A distraught **Natasha attempts suicide**.

The **French advance into Russia** as far as the Bolkonsky estate. **Andrei's father dies** as they get there and the **peasants turn on Maria**, but Nikolai Rostov, who is passing by, saves her. The ensuing **Battle of Borodino** ends in a stalemate; the Russians withdraw and the French advance on Moscow. **Andrei** is **wounded**. Pierre sees the slaughter and resolves to **assassinate Napoleon** but is **imprisoned**, meeting **Karataev**, a peasant who gives Pierre a renewed **sense of meaning**. The Rostovs flee Moscow, **leaving their possessions**, and help convey the wounded. Andrei, who is among them, **forgives Natasha before dying**. **Hélène dies** and **Pierre realizes that he loves Natasha**.

The epilogue sees the **wedding of Pierre and Natasha**, and Nikolai's marriage to Maria, whose wealth helps **relieve the Rostovs of their debts**.

JANE EYRE

Written by English novelist **Charlotte Brontë** (1816–55) and published in 1847, *Jane Eyre* is **a groundbreaking coming-of-age novel**. Among its revolutionary features is Charlotte Brontë's **rejection of the beautiful, docile heroine**, its **intimate first-person narrative style**, and the themes of **equality, class,** and **sexuality**.

Orphaned Jane Eyre grows up at **Gateshead Hall** with a cruel aunt, whose children **torment** Jane. She is sent away to a charity school, **Lowood,** where she is **treated harshly** by the abusive owner **Mr Brocklehurst**. Jane befriends **Helen Burns**, who endures her situation with **acceptance and grace**. Jane accidentally breaks a writing slate and is **branded a liar** and made to stand on a stool for an entire day. The benevolent superintendent **Mrs Temple** helps to **vindicate** Jane of the charges against her.

A **typhus** epidemic strikes the school. Helen contracts **tuberculosis** and **dies in Jane's arms**. An inquiry is carried out, shaming Mr Brocklehurst. Lowood changes dramatically and Jane becomes a **teacher**. She leaves after two years and becomes a **governess** at **Thornfield Hall**, tutoring the eight-year-old **Adèle**.

On a tour of the house, Jane hears an **eerie laugh**; the housekeeper says it is their peculiar servant **Grace Poole**.

During a walk, Jane helps a man who has been **thrown from his horse**. He is the mysterious owner of Thornfield and Adèle's guardian, **Mr Rochester**. One night, **she saves him from a fire** he claims was started by Grace Poole. The next day, Rochester leaves Thornfield to attend a party. **Jane realizes that she is falling in love** with him, but **Rochester returns with the beautiful socialite Blanche Ingram**.

Jane leaves to care for her dying aunt. On returning, Rochester **deceives Jane** by telling her he will marry Blanche and must let Jane go. In reality, **he has fallen in love with Jane**. He goads her into admitting how she feels, then **confesses his love** for her and **proposes**. However, their wedding is interrupted by Mr Mason, who **reveals Rochester is married to Mason's sister, Bertha**. Rochester explains that **Bertha has gone mad**, and that he pays Grace Poole to nurse her.

Jane flees Thornfield and is taken in by the Rivers family. Clergyman St. John Rivers proposes to her and she nearly accepts, but then hears **Rochester calling her**. She races back to Thornfield to find it has been burned to the ground by Bertha, **who has died in the fire**. **Rochester** saved his servants but **lost a hand and his vision**. Jane and Rochester reconcile and Rochester's eyesight recovers enough to see his **firstborn son**.

TESS OF THE D'URBERVILLES

Written by English novelist **Thomas Hardy** (1840–1928) and published in 1891, *Tess of the d'Urbervilles* is renowned for its **criticism of social injustice and sexual morality** in Victorian England.

Impoverished peddler **John Durbeyfield** discovers he is related to the noble **d'Urberville family**. Meanwhile, his 16-year-old daughter Tess is at the **May Dance**, where she encounters **Angel Clare**, the well-educated son of a reverend. Tess's mother hatches a plan for Tess to travel to the d'Urbervilles and **"claim kin"** to alleviate their financial worries.

At the d'Urberville estate, Tess meets **the cad Alec d'Urberville**, who is captivated by her beauty and finds her a **job** there. After Alec rescues Tess from a **confrontation**, they get lost in **dense fog**. Alec leaves to find help and returns to find Tess asleep. It is implied that Alec rapes Tess: "…temporarily blinded by his ardent manners, (Tess) had been stirred to confused surrender awhile." **Tess becomes pregnant**, returns to her family, and **gives birth** to a baby boy, who she names **Sorrow**. **The baby dies** shortly afterward.

A year later, Tess takes a job as a milkmaid at a dairy where she **falls in love with Angel Clare**. She accepts his **marriage proposal**, but tormented by her "indiscretion," she slides a

confessional letter under his door, but he never receives it. After the two are married, they **admit their sexual past**, with Angel confessing to an **affair**. **Tess forgives Angel, but he finds himself unable to forgive her**.

Angel departs for **Brazil** and Tess returns home, taking another job at a farm. She soon **encounters Alec again**, who has become a **minister**. He pursues Tess but she eventually **strikes him** for insulting Angel. Tess learns that both her parents are **ill** and returns home; **her father dies** and the family is **evicted** from their cottage. **Alec offers to help**, and convinced by Alec that Angel has abandoned her forever, **she accepts**.

Angel returns and finds Tess living with Alec. **Angel begs her to take him back**, but she tells him it is too late. She furiously confronts Alec and **stabs him in the heart**. She flees and finds Angel. He forgives her and they make plans to leave the country. **They hide in an abandoned mansion**, for a few days of **bliss**, but are discovered, and take off again.

They reach **Stonehenge** and Tess falls asleep after making **Angel promise** to **marry her sister** after Tess dies. They wake up surrounded by **police** and the book ends as a **black flag** is raised above Wintoncester prison, signaling that Tess has been executed.

FRANKENSTEIN

Frankenstein; or, The Modern Prometheus was written by English novelist **Mary Shelley** (1797–1851) and published in **1818**.

In the summer of 1816, **Percy Shelley**, **Lord Byron**, Percy's lover Mary, and others were staying with Byron at **Villa Diodati** near Lake Geneva. One candlelit evening, as a **thunderstorm** raged outside, Byron **suggested the group should each write ghost stories**. *Frankenstein* was Mary's idea, and became one of the most **influential** 19th-century novels. It is sometimes credited as the **first science fiction book**.

The book tells the tale of **Victor Frankenstein**, a student of science who becomes obsessed with finding the **secret of life**. He successfully **reanimates a body** fashioned from various parts of corpses, but is **horrified by his creation** and flees.

He falls gravely ill and is nursed by his childhood friend **Henry Clerval**; meanwhile the "creature" has **escaped**. When he recovers, Victor learns that **his brother William** has been **strangled to death**. On his journey home, Victor spots the creature and convinces himself he has **found the murderer**.

The family's housekeeper is accused of the murder and hanged. Filled with **anguish** and **guilt**, Victor travels to the **mountains** but is **pursued by the creature,** who confronts him and demands that Victor **creates a female companion** for him. The creature promises to disappear if Victor agrees but vows his **destruction** if he declines.

Victor agrees but catches sight of the creature watching him work and **destroys his half-built creation**. Following this, the creature vows **revenge**, promising that he "**will be with him on his wedding night.**" That night, Victor dumps the body of the second creature. Upon returning, he learns of his friend **Henry's murder by strangulation**.

Victor returns to Geneva and **marries his lover, Elizabeth**. He arms himself, leaves Elizabeth in her room, and searches the house and grounds for the creature. Meanwhile, the creature enters Elizabeth's room and **strangles her**. **Victor's father dies** shortly afterward of the grief.

Victor **pursues the creature** to the Arctic Circle, but collapses from **exhaustion** and is rescued by the explorer, **Captain Robert Walton**. **However, Victor soon dies**.

Walton finds the creature **mourning his creator's death**. The creature tells Walton of his **suffering, self-loathing**, and **remorse**. **He vows suicide** before drifting off on an ice raft into the distance.

MOBY DICK

Written by American novelist **Herman Melville** (1819–91) and published in **1851**, *Moby Dick* is regarded as one of the great American novels. The story was inspired by Melville's four-year-long voyage on the whaling ship *Acushnet* from 1841–45.

The novel starts with the famous line **"Call me Ishmael,"** which introduces its narrator. Ishmael meets and befriends kind Polynesian harpooner **Queequeg** and they travel to Nantucket to **seek work on a whaling ship**, finding employment aboard the *Pequod*.

The ship sets sail on Christmas Day and Ishmael learns about the mysterious ship's captain, **Ahab**, who only appears on deck several days into the voyage. Ahab is a grim-looking man, with a prosthetic leg fashioned from the **jaw of a sperm whale**, and he has a **white scar** running from his face down his entire body.

Ahab declares his mission of **vengeance** against **Moby Dick**, the accursed **white whale that nearly killed him**. Only first mate **Starbuck**, a pragmatic Quaker, questions the captain's feverish determination.

The *Pequod's* journey is punctuated by nine **"gams"**—social meetings with other ships on the open ocean.

After they gam with the *Samuel Enderby*, Ahab discovers the captain **lost his right arm** to Moby Dick. Queequeg falls ill and seems certain to die, with the ship's carpenter preparing him a **coffin**, but Queequeg **miraculously recovers**. After their two last gams, with the *Rachel* and *Delight*, both of which have suffered **fatal encounters** with Moby Dick, Ahab finally spots the whale.

On the first day of the chase, Moby Dick **bites Ahab's harpoon boat in two** and scatters the crew. On the second day, Ahab's harpooner, **Fedallah**, gets **entangled in a harpoon line** and is **dragged to his death**, lashed to the back of Moby Dick. On the third day, **Ahab's harpoon hits its mark** but he is **caught around the neck** by the line and **pulled under**. **Moby Dick** rams the *Pequod*, which **sinks**, and in the ensuing **vortex, all the men are lost**.

Ishmael, meanwhile, had been thrown from the boat and was far enough away to survive the whirlpool. Queequeg's coffin is **expelled from the depths**, on which Ishmael **floats** for a day and half until he is **rescued** by the *Rachel*.

THE GREAT GATSBY

Written by American novelist **F. Scott Fitzgerald** (1896–1940) and published in **1925**, *The Great Gatsby* is set in the decadent 1920s and charts the journey of outsider **Nick Carraway**, a **Midwestern** bond broker, who rents a house in a Long Island town characterized by **nouveau-riche** inhabitants.

Nick's cousin **Daisy** and her brutish husband **Tom Buchanan** live across the water in the **upper-class East Egg**. Nick learns that Tom has a mistress, **Myrtle Wilson**, wife of garage owner George, in a deprived area between New York and West Egg. Nick meets golfer **Jordan Baker**, and the two begin a romance.

Nick's neighbor, the enigmatic **Jay Gatsby**, lives in a **vast mansion** renowned for **outrageous parties**. Nick becomes entranced by Gatsby and receives an **invitation** to attend a party. At the party a man tells Nick he looks familiar and discovers they both **served in the same division** during **World War I**. At this point, Gatsby introduces himself. He is formal and **curiously indifferent** to his guests.

Nick and Gatsby become friends and Nick learns that Gatsby and Daisy had been **lovers** in 1917, when Gatsby was a **poor soldier**. Daisy had **promised to wait for him** to come back from France but later married Tom. Gatsby, who has amassed **vast wealth illegally**, lives on the other side of the bay to Daisy, and

hopes she will appear at one of his parties. He stares at the **green light** of her dock, **but she never comes**.

Gatsby persuades Nick to arrange a **"chance meeting"** with Daisy at Nick's house. They reunite and their love grows. One day, Nick and Gatsby travel to the Buchanans and the group makes for the city. Tom realizes that **Daisy loves Gatsby** and confronts him, **exposing him** as an **alcohol bootlegger**. Gatsby announces that Daisy is going to leave Tom, but Tom knows that her **shallow need** for the **security** that Tom's **class** brings her **trumps Gatsby's love**.

Daisy and Gatsby drive back to Long Island. Nick, Jordan, and Tom follow in Tom's coupé and come across an **accident**. **Myrtle has been killed** by a car, which it transpires **Daisy was driving**. **Tom tells George that Gatsby was responsible**. George becomes convinced that Gatsby was Myrtle's lover, **shooting Gatsby dead** before killing himself. Nick holds a poorly attended **funeral** for Gatsby, and reflects on the morally reprehensible, vacuous lives of Long Islanders and the **disintegration of the American Dream**. The novel ends with the line: "So **we beat on, boats against the current, borne back ceaselessly into the past**," highlighting the futile struggle to rekindle the past when we have forever been **corrupted by greed and deceit**.

NINETEEN EIGHTY-FOUR

Written by English novelist **George Orwell** (1903–50) and published in **1949**, *Nineteen Eighty-Four* is a **dystopian novel** about the **dangers of totalitarianism**. As one of the 20th century's most influential books, many of its features have entered popular culture, including **Big Brother**, the **Thought Police**, and **Room 101**.

The novel begins in London, the main city of **Airstrip One** in the superstate of **Oceania**, which is locked in a perpetual war with the other two world superstates. Oceania is governed by the **"Party,"** whose omniscient leader **"Big Brother"** is a ubiquitous presence on **telescreens** (two-way televisions) in a world where everyone is monitored and under surveillance of the authoritarian **Thought Police**.

The protagonist, **Winston Smith**, is a minor official who works in the **Ministry of Truth**, tasked with rewriting past editions of newspapers. As the book begins, Winston is contemplating whether to open a **diary** that he bought from a junk shop in a **proletarian** part of London, where the party **does not exercise complete control**. Winston knows that he will be **executed if he is caught with the diary**. However, he finds that the telescreen in his living room has moved, and a part of the room is out of its range. He uses this

alcove to **hide the diary** containing his **rebellious thoughts**.

Winston catches the gaze of a **senior Party official named O'Brien** and suspects he belongs to the resistance group, the **Brotherhood**. He notices **Julia**, a female colleague, staring at him. Despite fearing she is an **informant**, they begin an **affair** and rent an apartment above the junk shop. O'Brien initiates a conversation with Winston and invites him to his apartment.

Winston and Julia travel to O'Brien's apartment, where they tell him they **suspect** he is a **member** of the Brotherhood and ask to join him. He agrees and sends Winston a copy of the Brotherhood's **manifesto**, which he and Julia read. Suddenly, the pair are **seized** and taken to the **Ministry of Love** for **questioning**.

O'Brien is revealed as a **Party spy** and spends months **torturing Winston**. He is finally taken to **Room 101**, where his **worst fears are imagined**. O'Brien forces a wire cage onto Winston's head filled with **starving rats**, threatening to let them devour his face. He cannot cope anymore and cries out: **"Do it to Julia."** Their spirits broken, Winston and Julia are both released, now completely **brainwashed**. They meet but feel nothing. Winston has now **learned to love Big Brother**.

LORD OF THE FLIES

Written by British novelist **William Golding** (1911–93) and published in **1954**, *Lord of the Flies* tells the story of a group of **schoolboys marooned on an island**. It charts their descent into **savagery** and explores the **darker side of human nature**.

Two of the boys, the athletic **Ralph** and a bespectacled overweight boy nicknamed **Piggy**, find a conch that Ralph uses to assemble everyone. Ralph suggests they **elect a chief**, and Jack, the head boy and choir leader, suggests himself. However, they **elect Ralph**, who **appeases** Jack by **making the choir members the hunters of the group**.

Jack suggests they **use Piggy's glasses to light a fire** and **snatches them** from his face. Jack begins to **wrest control** from Ralph, suggesting they keep a fire lit to send **smoke signals** to rescuers. They treat Piggy as an **outcast**, but he is defended by kind-hearted Simon.

The younger boys develop a fear of an island **"beast,"** which Ralph insists does not exist, but Jack vows to **hunt it down**. To Ralph's dismay, a **ship** passes by the island, but Jack's group aren't manning the fire. Jack's band arrives, chanting in a **tribal frenzy**, brandishing sticks and carrying a pig carcass. In the ensuing confrontation, **Jack breaks Piggy's glasses** but apologizes for not supervising the fire; **order** is restored.

A plane **is shot down** and the pilot ejects, but is dead when his parachute lands. The twins manning the fire see the body and **mistake it for the "beast,"** alerting the others. Ralph, Jack, and his ally Roger try to find it and, although Ralph turns back earlier than the others, all three see the parachute and **believe they've seen the "beast."** Jack tries to **remove Ralph** as chief for his **cowardice**, but no one backs him.

Jack forms a **separate group**, which becomes increasingly **ritualistic**. They **slaughter a sow** and **put its head on a stick**. Simon comes across the fly-covered sow's head and hallucinates, with the **"Lord of the Flies"** telling him that the **"beast" exists inside all the boys**. Simon discovers the pilot, and returns to tell the group. However, they are in the middle of a **frenzied dance**, and **mistake Simon** for the beast, **killing him** with their teeth and hands.

Recognizing their value, Jack's band steal Piggy's glasses. Jack and Ralph **fight**, but Piggy interrupts them, brandishing the conch and demanding to be heard. Roger pushes a huge rock onto Piggy, **killing him** and **breaking the conch**. Ralph **escapes**, but **Jack's tribe hunt him and set fire to the forest**. Ralph trips, landing at the feet of a **British officer** alerted by the fire. The boys realize what they've done and **weep**.

DAVID COPPERFIELD

Written by English novelist **Charles Dickens** (1812–70) and published in **1849–50**, *David Copperfield* is written in the **first person** and charts the youth of the eponymous David, and parts of the novel **mirrors Dickens's own life**.

David's early years in Suffolk are happy, living with his mother and his nurse, Peggotty, until his mother marries the abusive **Edward Murdstone** when David is eight. During one beating, David **bites Murdstone's hand**, so he is sent to **Salem House** school under the charge of **Mr Creakle**. There he begins a friendship with **James Steerforth**, a bright boy who is a few years older than David.

David's **mother dies**, and Murdstone sends David to work for his wine business in London. He lodges with the charmingly cheery yet financially hopeless **Mr Micawber**, who is soon arrested and sent to a **debtor's prison**. With nowhere to turn, David walks from London to Dover to seek out his only relative—his eccentric aunt **Betsey Trotwood**, who takes him in, treats him kindly, and sends him to a good school run by **Dr Strong**.

While at school, he stays with **Mr Wickfield** and meets devious secretary **Uriah Heep** and Wickfield's angelic daughter, **Agnes**, who David becomes very close to. Heep starts to **control the fiscal affairs** of the alcoholic Wickfield. David joins the London law firm Spenlow and Jorkins and meets the beautiful but childish **Dora**, Spenlow's daughter, and **falls in love** at first sight. Betsey vists David and tells him that she faces **financial ruin**, which has largely been the **nefarious work of Uriah Heep**, who, to David's dismay, has Mr Micawber working for him. David takes clerical and writing work to help alleviate Betsey's situation, which, with the support of Agnes, leads to David becoming a **well-known writer**. It is Micawber who finally **exposes Uriah Heep's fraud**, allowing Betsey to regain some of her lost money.

David and Dora marry, but Dora never recovers from a miscarriage and dies. David travels to Yarmouth where he witnesses a **shipwreck** in which **Steerforth is killed**. Following these **tragedies, he travels abroad** for three years. Realizing **he loves Agnes, who secretly loves him**, David travels to England and reunites with her. He encounters the still scheming Uriah Heep, **imprisoned for bank fraud**.

Agnes and David marry and have children. **David finishes the book he's been writing about his life**, and the faces from his memories fade away except for one, Agnes, "**shining on me like a heavenly light**."

MIDNIGHT'S CHILDREN

Midnight's Children, written by British-Indian novelist **Salman Rushdie** (1947–), and published in **1981**, is an allegorical novel about **Indian independence** told by **Saleem Sinai** to Padma, his housekeeper.

Two babies are **born** in **Bombay** at **midnight** on August 15, 1947—the day of **Indian independence**. It transpires that all babies born between 12–1am that night—**midnight's children**—have **magical powers**. A midwife, **Mary Pereira**, switches the babies' nametags so that one—**Saleem**—is raised by **Ahmed** and **Amina** in a prosperous Muslim household. The other—**Shiva**—is brought up in **poverty**. Wracked with guilt, Mary becomes **Saleem's nanny**.

Prophecies were made about Saleem's birth so much is expected of him, but he struggles to cope and takes to hiding. One day he's punished with enforced silence for an entire day. He discovers he is a **telepath** and can **communicate with the other midnight's children**.

When Saleem **loses part of his finger** his parents discover that his blood type does not match theirs and he is not their son. Saleem is sent to live with his **Uncle Hanif**, but soon after he returns to his parents, **Hanif kills himself**. Mary confesses to swapping the boys at birth. Ahmed becomes a violent drunk, so Amina moves Saleem and his sister to **Pakistan** to live with aunt **Emerald** and her husband **General Zulfikar**.

In Pakistan, Zulfikar orchestrates a **coup d'état**, which Saleem witnesses. Four years pass, during which time **India lose a war to China**. Saleem has an **operation** to clear his sinuses, causing him to **lose his telepathy**, but he learns he can **detect the smell of emotions**.

War breaks out between India and Pakistan, and **all of Saleem's family is killed**, except Saleem, and his younger sister. A bomb causes a **spittoon** to hit Saleem's head, causing **amnesia**. He is **conscripted** into the Pakistan army but flees to the jungle where he is **bitten by a snake**; he regains his memory.

Saleem meets **Parvati-the-witch**, a midnight's child who smuggles him into India. She has an affair with Shiva, now an adulterous war hero, and falls pregnant. Parvati is shunned so Saleem **consents to marry her**. In India, **Indira Gandhi** instigates a **sterilization campaign**, targeting midnight's children. Government forces, led by Shiva, kill Parvati and capture Saleem, forcing him to identify the midnight's children, who are **rounded up** and **sterilized**.

Saleem eats some **chutney** that tastes like one Mary used to make. He travels to the factory, which it turns out Mary owns. **Saleem marries Padma** on the 31st anniversary of India's independence but they get lost in a crowd and **Saleem is trampled into dust**, like, he reflects, **all the future midnight's children will be**.

CHAPTER

2

POLITICS

PHILOSOPHY

& ECONOMICS

PLATO'S THE REPUBLIC

The Greek philosopher **Plato** (c. 428–348 BC) was one of the most **influential thinkers** in history. He was a devoted follower of the philosopher Socrates (c. 469–399 BC) and he taught **Aristotle** (c. 384–22 BC) at the **Academy** that he founded just outside **Athens**.

This triumvirate comprises the three most **important figures in the foundation of Western philosophy**.

Plato's most famous work, *The Republic*, was written around 380 BC and is structured as a conversation between several characters, the most important of which is Socrates. This method of writing became known as **Socratic Dialogue**, and it involves a process of **interrogation to find fault and inconsistencies in another person's reasoning** in order to **reveal the path to wisdom**.

In *The Republic*, Plato attempts to understand the **meaning of justice** by defining it and then analyzing how it functions in **contemporary societies**. He "proposes" that this debate can be furthered by examining the potential features of an **"ideal state."**

Plato introduces three classes of people—guardians, or **rulers**; auxiliaries or **soldiers**; and producers, or **farmers/craftsmen**—and states that each group must perform a **specific societal function** according to their skills. Citizens can be said to live in a **"just state"** so long as they honor these functions and **do not encroach on the rights of other citizens**. This agreement to be temperate is effectively a **social contract** that allows citizens to be residents in a **harmonious society**.

Plato makes the point that a just society and a just individual **share certain parallels**. Each person has **three parts, mirroring the three classes**: appetites, spirits, and rational faculties, and these must be correctly structured to ensure a just soul. The rational part has to **rule**, while the spirited part **upholds the convictions** of the rational part, while the part representing "appetites" must **obey**.

Plato establishes that in the ideal state, it is the **philosopher** who is the most just individual and as such is the **ideal ruler** of the just city.

THE COMMUNIST MANIFESTO

The Communist Manifesto was a pamphlet written by German philosopher **Karl Marx** (1818–83) and **Friedrich Engels** (1820–95) and published on behalf of the **Communist League** on **February 21, 1848**.

It is **the most influential document about socialism** in existence, written at a time when a huge **underclass of workers** across Europe lived and worked in **abject conditions without political representation**.

The Communist Manifesto argues that the history of mankind to this point has been characterized by a **class struggle** between the **bourgeoisie, the capitalist ruling class** who control the raw materials, tools, and machines (known as the **"means of production"**), and the **proletariat—the exploited and oppressed class** whose only material value is their ability to work.

The Manifesto calls for an **overthrow** of these conditions, whereby the **proletariat will rise up in revolution against the bourgeoisie**. It ends with the famous line: "The proletarians have nothing to lose but their chains. They have a world to win. **Working men of all countries, unite."**

Marx theorized that the revolution would usher in a period of **socialism** where the **means of production are returned to the workers and private property ceases to exist**. The final stage is **Communism**, where both classes and the state itself are abolished, and replaced by a system where the people administer their own lives and each person contributes and receives according to their needs.

The Manifesto had **predicted that revolution would take place in Europe**; in France, this began the day after the Manifesto was published, but it was unconnected to the pamphlet's release, which was initially written in German. By February 24, the **French king, Louis-Philippe, had been overthrown**, and an **insurrection** took place in **Berlin** in March. Unrest spread throughout Europe, but, with the exception of France, governments weathered the storm.

Sixty-nine years later, in **November 1917**, the Russian proletariat in St Petersburg rose up and overthrew the Tsarist government, led by **Vladimir Lenin** and inspired by his interpretation of Marx's ideology.

TIMELINE OF WOMEN'S SUFFRAGE

With few exceptions, **women were historically denied the ability to vote in elections** until the 19th century. In the **UK** in **1869, single women property owners** were granted the **vote in local elections,** but it would take nearly half a century for further progress toward equal voting rights with men.

In **1832,** the first petition was presented to the UK Parliament on behalf of Yorkshirewoman **Mary Smith,** who stated that "she paid taxes, and therefore did not see why she should not have a share in the election of a Representative." The idea was laughed out of the House of Commons.

Philosopher and MP **John Stuart Mill** (1806–73) brought a petition to Parliament in **1866** with **1,499 signatures** calling for votes for women, which led to the first parliamentary debate the following year.

It was **New Zealand that became the first self-governing country to allow women the vote** in parliamentary elections in **1893,** after years of campaigning led by suffragette **Kate Sheppard** (1847–1934). In **1902,** women's suffrage was extended across all of **Australia.**

Frustrated with the lack of movement in the UK by peaceful means, in 1903 **Emmeline Pankhurst** founded the **Women's Social and Political Union,** committed to **"Deeds, not words."** Members **attacked police officers,** detonated **explosive devices,** and committed **arson,** deeming that the only way to win the vote was through violence.

In 1913, suffragette **Emily Davison** stepped out in front of the king's horse at the **Epsom Derby.** This action and her subsequent death from her injuries made **international headlines.**

In 1918, the UK granted women **over 30** the vote **provided they** (or their husband) **met certain property requirements.** The same year, a law was passed allowing women to stand as MPs. In the 1918 General Election, one woman—**Constance Markievicz**—was elected as MP for the Dublin St Patrick's constituency. Finally, the **Representation of the People Act 1928,** gave women the same voting rights as men in the UK.

In the **United States,** 1920 saw the ratification of the **19th Amendment,** granting women the right to vote.

Saudi Arabia was the last country to give women the vote, in **2015.**

THE ORIGINS OF THE ARAB–ISRAELI CONFLICT

The origin of the **conflict between Arab nations and Israel** stems from the **religious** and **political significance** of **Palestine**. The **Hebrew Bible** promises the Jewish people the **right to claim their ancestral home in Palestine**, a land of **sacred religious** and **historical significance** to **Muslims**, which has been inhabited by an **Arab Muslim majority** since the **12th century**.

The Jewish claim to their ancestral homeland evolved into an **organized political movement** known as **Zionism**, spearheaded by Austrian journalist **Theodor Herzl** in the late 19th century.

In the wake of **escalating persecution of the Jews** in Russia in the early 20th century, the **British Secretary of State for the Colonies, Joseph Chamberlain**, proposed a solution in **1903**. He offered to **provide land in East Africa**, but the **"Uganda Scheme"** was **rejected** by the **Zionist Congress** in 1905.

After six months of **stalemate** fighting the **Ottoman forces in 1917**, the British defeated a combined German and Ottoman army at the **Battle of Beersheba** on **October 31, 1917**, ushering in an era of British rule

that lasted until 1947. **Capitalizing on the military success** and **keen to win over the international Jewish community** to the **Allied** cause, on **November 2** the British Foreign Secretary **Sir Arthur James Balfour** wrote a public letter to **Lord Rothschild**, a Jewish MP and organizer of the Zionist cause in Great Britain. In the letter, which became known as the **Balfour Declaration**, Balfour announced the government's official support for **establishing Palestine as a "national home for the Jewish people."**

On **November 29, 1947**, the UN recommended the adoption of a plan to **partition Palestine** into **independent Arab and Jewish states,** with **Jerusalem administered** by an **international trusteeship**.

Civil war broke out, which became an **interstate conflict** on **May 15, 1948**, following **David Ben-Gurion's establishment of the State of Israel** the day before.

Despite brief periods of peace, **the Arab–Israeli conflict continues to this day.**

APARTHEID

Apartheid is an Afrikaans word meaning **"apartness,"** describing **institutionalized racial segregation** and **discrimination** against **South Africa's non-white population.**

Apartheid became **official policy** after the National Party won the **1948 General Election,** but in reality, informal racial division existed from the early days of Dutch colonial rule.

The first apartheid laws enacted were the **1949 Prohibition of Mixed Marriages Act** and the **1950 Immorality Act,** which **outlawed interracial marriage** and sexual relations. The **1950 Population Registration Act** classified people as **White, Bantu** (black Africans), and **Colored** (mixed race). A fourth category, for **Asians,** was added later.

In 1952, the **Natives Act** was introduced (known as the **Pass Laws**), which made it mandatory for black South Africans over the age of 16 to carry a **"reference book"** containing personal information. They were often forced to violate the laws to find work, so **arrests** were a **constant threat.**

In 1953, the **Reservation of Separate Amenities Act segregated public spaces according to race.** The next stage involved the creation of 10 **Bantustans** (tribal homelands) in 1959 and the **forced removal of black Africans from their homes** to unfamiliar areas set

aside by the government. The citizens of Bantustans would no longer be South African by nationality, and from 1960–82 approximately 3.5 million black Africans underwent **forced migration.**

The **international community condemned the atrocities** occurring in South Africa. The UK and US imposed **economic sanctions** and the country was **thrown out of the Commonwealth.** Domestically, the African National Congress (ANC) had instigated a campaign of **civil disobedience** back in the 1950s, but in **1960,** after the South African Police **killed 69 students** demonstrating against the Pass Laws Act during the **Sharpesville massacre,** protests turned violent. Bowing to growing pressure, the National Party **repealed the Pass Laws in 1986** and gave non-whites the right to own property and join provincial governments.

In **1991** there was a more historic shift in policy with **President F. W. de Klerk scrapping the remaining apartheid laws.** A new interim constitution took effect in 1994, and national elections, open to all races, were held. The **ANC won 62%** of the vote and **Nelson Mandela** was elected as **President,** four years after his release from 27 years' imprisonment for **conspiring to overthrow the state.**

WATERGATE

Watergate was the name given to the **biggest political scandal in US history**. On **June 17, 1972, five men broke** into the **headquarters of the Democratic National Committee** at the **Watergate office complex** in **Washington D.C.** The investigation that followed revealed a **cover-up** that led all the way to the White House and resulted in the **resignation of President Richard Nixon**.

The FBI investigations that followed revealed that four of the burglars had **CIA connections** and that one of them was a security coordinator for the **Republican National Committee** and the **Committee for Re-election of the President**.

Meanwhile, during the campaign for the **1972 Presidential election,** *The Washington Post* reporters **Bob Woodward** and **Carl Bernstein** began to receive information from an anonymous source using the pseudonym **"Deep Throat"** that revealed the extent of the cover-up (many years later, in 2005, the mystery voice was revealed to be that of **FBI Deputy Director, Mark Felt**).

Despite several revelatory **scoops** appearing on the front page of *The Washington Post*, the White House convinced the public that the

newspaper was pursuing a **vendetta** against President Nixon. His public image was undamaged and he **won the election by a landslide**.

After the **trial of the burglars** in **January 1973** made it clear that many questions remained unanswered, the **Senate** voted to form **a select committee to investigate Watergate**. The **revelations it uncovered** included **Nixon's secret audio recordings** of his conversations with his officials, which the **Supreme Court ordered to be released** in **July 1974**. One recording became known as the **"Smoking Gun"** tape, as it revealed that on June 23, 1972, Nixon **requested that the FBI halt the investigation** into Watergate. **He had been part of the criminal conspiracy since the beginning**.

With **impeachment** proceedings looming, **Nixon resigned on television on August 9, 1974**, with vice-president **Gerald Ford** being sworn in as President later that day. A month later, **Ford controversially pardoned Nixon for his involvement in the Watergate scandal**.

Watergate became such a commonly used synonym for scandal that the US and international press began adding the suffix **"-gate"** to scandals, a legacy that continues to this day.

KEYNESIAN ECONOMICS AND MONETARISM

British economist **John Maynard Keynes** (1883–1946) revolutionized the economic policies of Western governments during the **1930s** until the 1970s. He took an alternative approach to the **classical economic theory** that financial markets will right themselves during **downturns** and **do not require government intervention**. The **Great Depression** of the 1930s challenged this accepted "free market" notion, because the markets did not return to an equilibrium point—**unemployment remained high** and **output** was low.

Keynes theorized that to remedy the effects of a recession, **the government should increase expenditure and create debt** in order to maintain demand and **stop rising unemployment**. Once the economy recovered, **the debt could be repaid**. Correspondingly, during periods of prolonged growth, a government must **increase taxation or cut spending, creating a surplus**. Keynesian economics became standard policy in most of the world's major economies after **World War II** and is widely credited for helping the **sustained post-war boom**.

Monetarism became the dominant school of thought during the tough conditions of the **1970s**, when **growth stagnated** and **unemployment** and **inflation rose**. Keynesian economics

no longer seemed to work, so a new approach was called for.

Monetarism was pioneered by US economist **Milton Friedman** (1912–2006), who believed that regulating the **supply of money** was the **key to economic growth**. He posited that issuing too much money would make its value drop, in other words, create inflation. Instead, he theorized that the supply of money **should automatically rise each year** at a rate **linked to a country's Gross Domestic Product (GDP)**. He called this **Friedman's k-percent rule** and suggested that this was the way to ensure **consistent economic growth** with **low inflation**.

Monetarism famously became the central tenet of **Margaret Thatcher's** (1925–2013) economic policy, as an attempt to combat a period of **high inflation**, a **flagging industrial sector**, and the growing power of **trade unions**. **Interest rates** were **raised, taxes** were **increased** or introduced, including the controversial **poll tax**, and key public sector industries were **privatized**. While monetarist policy did **reduce inflation, unemployment** reached its highest point since the 1930s, **manufacturing output** weakened, and **wage inequality** grew. By **1984**, monetarist policy had been effectively **abandoned** in the UK.

CAUSES OF THE 2007–8 FINANCIAL CRISIS

The origins of the **2007–8 Financial Crisis** can arguably be **traced back to 2000** and the **bursting of the Dotcom Bubble**—the unsustainable period of **frenzied investment** in often vastly **overvalued Internet companies** that began in 1997. Within a year, the US and much of the developed world had entered **recession**.

The **Federal Reserve** responded by lowering **interest rates** to stimulate the economy, flooding the market with **"cheap" money** (loans or credit with a low interest rate). The economic fallout following the **terrorist attacks** on New York on September 11, 2001, resulted in further cuts to interest rates, which dipped to **1.25%** in **January 2002**, the lowest since **1948**.

In this economic climate, it became much easier to **buy a house**. Mortgage lenders began **approving mortgages** for **high-risk borrowers**, taking a **gamble** on the potential risks of the borrowers defaulting in favor of increased **potential profitability** as a result of charging them higher interest rates. These **"subprime" borrowers** often took out significantly **larger loans than they could afford**, assuming that rising housing values meant that they would simply be able to sell their house at a higher price later on.

In 2004, home ownership in the US reached a peak of 70%. With **supply exceeding demand**, the bubble burst late in 2005 and **house prices began to fall**. At the same time, the Federal Reserve had grown increasingly concerned about **rising inflation** and **unemployment**, so they began to **increase interest rates**.

Between June 2004 and June 2006, the interest rate rose to **5.25%**, slowing the housing market. Many of the subprime borrowers were on **adjustable-rate mortgages** to avoid paying high initial rates and were unable to afford the increased payments, so they began **defaulting on their mortgages**.

In February and March 2007, the **US subprime mortgage market began to collapse** and 25 lenders filed for **bankruptcy**. The subprime crisis evolved into an **international financial crisis** in 2008, the economic effects of which are still being felt to this day.

The 2007–8 financial crisis is believed by many economists to be the **worst** since the **Great Depression** following the **Wall Street Crash** of **1929**.

EXISTENTIALISM

Jean Paul Sartre (1905–80) was a key figure in the loosely connected system of philosophical ideas referred to as **existentialism**. The term is believed to have originated with French philosopher **Gabriel Marcel** (1889–1973) in the mid-1940s, although the Danish philosopher **Søren Kierkegaard** (1813–55) is widely regarded as the **first existentialist philosopher**.

Existentialism centers on the **problematic nature of the human condition** and highlights the **key themes of the "absurd," dread (or angst), alienation, boredom, and nothingness**.

Sartre reversed the ancient idea that everything has a set of **fundamental characteristics** that make up what it is. He believed that humans live their lives and are **defined by their actions**, rather than some inherent pre-defined set of ideal characteristics. This is the heart of his famous expression **"existence precedes essence,"** which features in Sartre's masterpiece, ***Being and Nothingness*** (1943). In it, he also examines **the nature of consciousness**, suggesting that it does not make sense by itself, but can only be defined in relation to something else.

One of the key ideas in existentialism is that life is **absurd**, because the human attempt to find **meaning** and **value** in the world is frustrated by the absence of these concepts. Another key concept is **angst**, a Danish word meaning "dread" or "anxiety." Attributed to Kierkegaard, it focuses on the **fear** that comes with the **freedom to determine your own actions**. Kierkegaard used the example of **standing in front of a cliff edge with the choice between life and death**. This realization that you have control over your life, which he believed occurred in all of our choices, produces **dread**, something he referred to as the **"dizziness of freedom."**

Sartre and his lifelong companion, French intellectual **Simone de Beauvoir** (1908–86) were largely responsible for the **popularization of existentialism in the 1940s and 1950s**. De Beauvoir famously shaped Sartre's "existence precedes essence" into the feminist mantra: **"One is not born but becomes a woman"** in her groundbreaking novel ***The Second Sex***, published in 1949.

ALAN TURING AND THE TURING TEST

The brief but remarkable life of mathematician **Alan Turing** (1912–54) had a profound impact on the **history of computing**, the study of **artificial intelligence**, and the **success** of the **Allied War effort** during **World War II**.

On the first day of World War II, Turing started work at the Allied codebreaking center at **Bletchley Park**, tasked with **cracking** the **German Enigma code**. Turing's resulting electro-mechanical machine, the **Bombe**, was installed on **March 19, 1940**. By 1943, a network of Bombes was able to crack around **84,000** Enigma messages each month. A huge breakthrough included the cracking of the specific Enigma code used by **U-boats** allowing merchant convoys to **dodge submarine patrols** in the Atlantic. His pioneering work is widely believed to have **shortened the war**, potentially **saving millions of lives**.

In October 1950, Turing published a paper entitled ***Computing Machinery and Intelligence***. In it, he outlined a proposal to determine whether machines can demonstrate intelligent behavior. Referred to as **"the imitation game"** by Turing, it became better known as the **Turing Test**. The test asks whether a **human interrogator** can **distinguish between a human subject and a computer** based on their responses to a series of questions. The machine is successful if it causes the interrogator to mistakenly determine that the machine is the human. This became a **landmark experiment in the study of artificial intelligence**, a phrase that was only coined in 1956.

In 1952, Turing was arrested for **"gross indecency"** for his sexual relationship with a 19-year-old man. He was **convicted**, had his **security clearance revoked**, and underwent **chemical castration**, involving a year-long course of hormone injections which left him impotent. The involvement of this "treatment" in his death on June 7, 1954, is the source of **heated debate**, as is the cause of his death, which was officially recorded as **suicide**. A **half-eaten apple** was found on his bedside table, believed to be **laced with cyanide**, although the **police never tested for it**. It is possible that his death was an **accident** as he was conducting experiments with cyanide in his house at the time.

Contrary to popular belief, the design of the **Apple logo** was not inspired by Turing, with co-founder **Steve Jobs** admitting "God, we wish it were" in 2011.

CHAPTER

3

SCIENCE

ARCHIMEDES' "EUREKA" MOMENT

Archimedes (c. 287–12 BC) was an Ancient Greek **polymath**, credited with numerous crucial **scientific discoveries** and **inventions**, including his design for a screw pump used to raise water, which became known as the **Archimedes' Screw**. He also developed revolutionary **military machines** including the **"death ray"**— a system of **mirrors** used to **concentrate sunlight** in order to set fire to an enemy fleet.

However, Archimedes is best known for his discovery of a **law of buoyancy** that allowed him to **calculate the volume of an irregularly shaped object**. This discovery, which became known as Archimedes' Principle, is the origin of the expression **"Eureka!", literally meaning "I have found it!"**

The story goes that Archimedes was asked by **King Hiero II of Syracuse** to determine whether a **goldsmith** had used **pure gold** in a **crown** or whether he had added cheaper **silver**. While in the bathtub, Archimedes observed that **as his body sank into the water, the**

water level rose. He realized that the amount of water he displaced was an accurate measure of his volume, and he could **apply this principle to determine the volume of the crown**. He reasoned that **because gold weighs more than silver**, a crown mixed with silver would **need to be larger** to reach the same weight as one made of pure gold. Therefore, **the blended crown would displace more water than its pure gold counterpart**.

The legend is that this epiphany caused Archimedes to **leap out of the bath** and run home completely naked screaming **"Eureka!"**

The famous Eureka story was first written about 200 years after the event by author and architect **Vitruvius**, who included an account of it in his introduction to his treatise *De Architecture*. It is widely believed that while Archimedes' discovery was accurate, the "naked mathematician running excitedly through the streets" element may well have been a slight embellishment!

COPERNICUS'S HELIOCENTRIC MODEL

Nicolaus Copernicus (1474–1543) was a Polish astronomer who **transformed scientific thinking about the nature of the Solar System**. His most significant work, published in **1543**, was *De revolutionibus orbium coelestium* (*On the Revolutions of Heavenly Spheres*), in which he created a mathematical model of the **Sun** rather than the Earth as the **center of the Solar System**.

This idea, known as **heliocentrism**, is derived from the Greek word *helios* (meaning "sun") and was first outlined by the Ancient Greek astronomer **Aristarchus of Samos** (c. 310–230 BC). It challenged the established **Ptolemaic system**, which suggested that the Earth lies motionless at the center of the Solar System with the Sun, Moon, stars, and other planets revolving around it.

Copernicus had been working on his magnum opus since **1506** and had completed it by **1530**. It is speculated that he delayed publication until the year of his death (some accounts claim that he was presented with the final pages on his deathbed) for fear of condemnation by the Church, as the idea of heliocentrism contradicted the word of the Bible and was thus considered **heretical**. Copernicus actually **dedicated the book to Pope Paul III** to mitigate criticism that had already been mounted by figures such as **Martin Luther** (1483–1546), who had become aware of Copernicus's theory in 1539.

Luther famously wrote: "The fool wants to turn the whole art of astronomy upside-down. However, as Holy Scripture tells us, so did Joshua bid the Sun to stand still and not the Earth."

It took some time for the scientific and wider community to **accept the heliocentric model**, but Copernicus's work was later considered **a major milestone in the history of science**. It triggered the **Copernican Revolution**, which would have a major impact on the life and work of the astronomers **Johannes Kepler** (1571–1630) and **Galileo** (1564–1642).

CHARLES DARWIN'S ON THE ORIGIN OF SPECIES

Charles Darwin (1809–82) was an English naturalist who pioneered the study of **evolutionary biology** with his seminal book *On the Origin of Species* in 1859.

While Darwin was not the first scientist to write about evolution, he was the first to propose a theory that explained **how species adapt without involving God**. He gave this mechanism the name **natural selection**.

Darwin spent nearly five years aboard *HMS Beagle* as the ship's naturalist from 1831–6, a round-the-world expedition he called "by far the most important event of my life." The collections and observations he made on this journey **altered his belief that species were fixed**, providing the ingredients for his theory.

The theory of natural selection works like this. Imagine a population of beetles—some are **brown** and some **red**. The population cannot continue multiplying because there is not enough food in their environment to support them. The red beetles do not fare as well as the brown beetles because they are not well **camouflaged** against trees, so **tend to get eaten by birds**. So the red beetles **do not reproduce** as often as the brown ones. Because the **trait** of being brown in color is passed on **genetically**, the young of the surviving brown beetles are also brown. The color brown is a more **beneficial trait** than red, so it becomes more and more common in the beetle population until **eventually all the beetles are brown**. He called this **"descent with modification."**

Darwin's theory explains that the **diversity of life on Earth** came about via the process of descent with modification through a **vast branching pattern**. He famously drew up a **"tree of life"** to show that species are related through their evolutionary history.

FREUD AND PSYCHOANALYSIS

The Austrian neurologist **Sigmund Freud** (1856–1939) was the **founder of psychoanalysis**, a method of **treating mental health disorders** by examining the relationship between the **conscious** and **unconscious** parts of a person's mind. It was Freud who first used the term "psychoanalysis," in 1896, in reference to the treatment of neuroses.

Freud believed that unconscious factors were largely responsible for our **emotions** and **behavior**. Bringing these into consciousness was a **key part of his therapeutic approach** and involved finding the origins of these unconscious factors, many of which could be traced back to **childhood experiences**.

Three of the key factors in Freud's theory are the acknowledgment of **repression**, the significance of **sexual instinct**, and **transference**. To Freud, repression was understood as a **defense mechanism** that prevents disturbing

or threatening thoughts from entering the conscious mind.

According to Freud, sexual instinct—our innate desire to have sexual relations—is the **motivating force behind our behavior**. Transference, characterized by the unconscious **redirection of feelings and desires to another person**, was described by Freud as a vital part of treatment in psychoanalysis.

One of Freud's most significant theories was the idea that the human psyche comprises three aspects, which he called the **id**, **ego**, and **super-ego**. The id is the **primitive instinctual** aspect of the mind; the super-ego is a kind of **moral conscience**; and the ego functions as the **realistic** part that **mediates** between the **conflicting desires** of the id and the super-ego. The three parts together form the **complex behavior of humans**.

MARIE CURIE AND THE DISCOVERY OF RADIOACTIVITY

Marie Curie (1867–1934) was a Polish physicist and chemist who made groundbreaking scientific advances about **radioactivity**, a term that she coined. Shortly after she met the French physicist, and her future husband, **Pierre Curie** (1859–1906) in 1894 at the **Sorbonne** in Paris, they formed a **prolific scientific partnership**.

The Curies began exploring the invisible **rays** emanating from **uranium**. Investigations of a mineral known as **pitchblende** revealed an **unknown element** that appeared to be highly radioactive. In 1898, Marie and Pierre named this element **polonium**, after Marie's home country. Later that year, they discovered that pitchblende contained tiny quantities of another unknown element far more radioactive than polonium. Later, in 1898, they named the new element **radium**.

In 1903, together with **Henri Becquerel** (1852–1908), they were awarded the **Nobel Prize in Physics** for their pioneering work on **radiation**. Marie's contribution, however, was originally ignored by the nomination committee. It was only an intervention by a sympathetic member of the

committee that drew Pierre's attention to this glaring omission, leading him to write a letter clarifying that he only wished to be considered together with Marie. This was **the first time a woman had been awarded a Nobel Prize**.

In 1906, **Pierre was tragically killed** in a road accident. Marie was offered his post as **Professor of Physics at the Sorbonne**, becoming the first woman to teach there. Her pioneering work included **research into the treatment of cancer** using radioactive isotopes.

In 1911, she was **awarded the Nobel Prize for a second time**, this time for Chemistry, for her work on polonium and radium. In doing so, she became the **first person to win Nobel Prizes across more than one discipline**.

During World War I, Marie Curie developed **mobile radiography units** to help locate and remove shrapnel and bullets, which **treated thousands of soldiers and civilians**. Sadly, her **prolonged exposure to radiation** during her professional and war-time service caused chronic illnesses, and Marie died in 1934.

EINSTEIN'S LAWS OF RELATIVITY

The German theoretical physicist **Albert Einstein** (1879–1955) developed a theory in 1905, which would forever alter the landscape of science. The paper was originally called **"On the Electrodynamics of Moving Bodies,"** which he later referred to as the **Special Theory of Relativity** to distinguish it from his **General Theory of Relativity**.

It proposed an answer to the **contradiction** between the **laws of motion** and the **laws of electromagnetism**—the greatest mystery in physics at the time. The laws of motion dictated that the velocity of any object is relative to the velocity of other objects. However, according to the rules of electromagnetism, **light travels at a fixed speed**. How could both rules be true?

Einstein theorized that **as an object moves faster through space, it actually travels slower through time**, a phenomenon he called **time dilation**. This means that objects experience space and time differently, according to the velocity at which they are traveling. The closer they get to the speed of light, the slower time appears to move.

Einstein's Special Theory of Relativity was **incompatible with Issac Newton's description of gravity** in 1687. Einstein sought to address this by unifying his relativistic theory of space and time with gravity.

And so, in 1916, the General Theory of Relativity was born. In it, Einstein introduced the idea of **space–time**, the fusing of **three-dimensional space** and time into a **four-dimensional continuum**. He proposed that space–time is warped by huge objects, such as the Sun. It is this **warping effect** that creates the effects of gravity rather than a force of attraction.

THE MANHATTAN PROJECT

In the summer of 1939, Hungarian-German physicist **Leo Szilard** (1898–1964) convinced **Albert Einstein** (1879–1955), who had fled Germany and settled in the US, to write to American President **F. D. Roosevelt** (1882–1945) to **warn him** that **Nazi Germany may attempt to develop an atomic bomb**. The letter urged the President to speed up the atomic research being carried out in the US. Roosevelt's response was swift, setting up a Uranium Advisory Committee, which paved the way for the creation of what became known as the **Manhattan Project**.

The Manhattan Project, active between **1942–6**, was responsible for creating the first atomic bombs. The original cover name was the **Laboratory for the Development of Substitute Materials**, but this was later renamed Manhattan District as many of the early stages of the project were undertaken in New York.

In the end, over **30** different sites were used for production, research, and development across the US as well as in **Canada** and the **UK**, but the three primary sites were **Hanford, Washington; Oak Ridge, Tennessee;** and **Los Alamos, New Mexico.**

The first director of the secret Los Alamos Laboratory was **Robert Oppenheimer** (1904–67), who oversaw the development of two different types of nuclear weapon. The first was the **"gun-type,"** which worked by firing one mass of the isotope **uranium-235** into another; the second was the more complicated **"implosion-type,"** which used explosive charges to crush a plutonium sphere. The first atomic bomb, codenamed **"Trinity,"** was detonated at the **Alamogordo** air base in New Mexico on **July 16, 1945**.

On **August 6, 1945**, an atomic bomb codenamed **"Little Boy"** was dropped on **Hiroshima, Japan**. Three days later, the second atomic bomb, codenamed **"Fat Man,"** hit the city of **Nagasaki**. It is estimated that together both bombs killed **130,000–225,000** people. Japan **surrendered** six days later, marking the end of World War II, although many of the **ethical** and **legal** implications of the atomic bombings will be debated forever.

QUANTUM MECHANICS

Quantum mechanics is a theory that describes the behavior of **sub-atomic particles**. In "classical" mechanics, which studies the effects of forces and energy on the motion of everyday objects, particles exist in a specific location at a specific time. However, sub-atomic particles behave in completely different ways. For example, they can act like **waves** as well as **particles**.

It is also impossible to determine both their **precise position** and **velocity**. This is known as the **uncertainty principle**. So sub-atomic particles exist in a form of limbo—they effectively exist in all the possible positions they can be in at the same time. This in-between state is called **quantum superposition**. However, when the sub-atomic particles are **observed**, for example by an electronic detector, something very strange happens. The sub-atomic particle "decides" which position to be in, as if it has reverted to the type of behavior exhibited by normal particles.

Schrodinger's Cat is a famous thought experiment named after its creator, the **Nobel Prize-winning Austrian physicist**. It applies the principle of quantum superposition to a scenario involving regular objects. A cat is locked in a box containing a vial of **poison**, **radioactive material**, and a **Geiger counter**, used to detect radioactivity. If radiation is detected, the Geiger counter triggers a hammer to smash open the vial of poison and the cat dies. However, it is not possible to determine whether the cat is alive or dead until the box is opened, so the cat is simultaneously **both alive** and **dead** until that point.

It has so far been **impossible** to incorporate both quantum mechanics and general relativity into one consistent model. Creating a **unified** theory—a **theory of everything**—is the biggest challenge in modern physics.

THE HUMAN GENOME PROJECT

The Human Genome Project (HGP) was a major **international collaboration** to **map out** and **understand** the **entire makeup** of **human genes**.

The genetic information of every living thing is contained in molecules of deoxyribonucleic acid (DNA). **DNA** is made up of **four chemical compounds called "bases"**: adenine, thymine, guanine, and cytosine. Adenine joins with thymine and cytosine with guanine to form base pairs, which make up the building blocks of **DNA's famous double helix** structure, which looks a bit like a twisted ladder.

In all, there are around **3 million base pairs in each human**. All genes consist of stretches of these base pairs, arranged in different ways and in different lengths. The Human Genome Project determined the order of all the bases.

The HGP was officially launched in 1990 and the sequence was declared complete on **April 14, 2003**. It revealed that there are approximately **22,500 genes** present in the human genome—some small gaps remain that are unrecoverable with today's technology, but the genome is functionally complete for the purposes of scientific research.

One huge breakthrough of the HGP is that researchers can now **easily find genes suspected of causing inherited diseases**. The ability to predict the development of disease makes it possible to **medically intervene** to limit the damage a disease can do.

The HGP has also facilitated the work of **gene therapy**—the technique to treat disease by **inserting a healthy copy of a gene into a person's cells**. It has also revolutionized the study of **forensics**, enabling the identification of suspects from tiny samples of saliva, hairs, or dried blood.

THE LARGE HADRON COLLIDER

The Large Hadron Collider (LHC) is the world's **largest particle accelerator** and is used to investigate the fundamental constituents of matter. It comprises a **16¾-mile (27-km) ring** of **superconducting magnets** built at an average depth of **330 ft (100 m)**.

It was built between 1998 and 2008, and is located at the European Organization for Nuclear Research (**CERN**) laboratory on the France-Switzerland border near Geneva. The "hadron" in the title refers to the name of a composite particle, which is categorized into two families, one of which includes protons. The "large" in the title is due to the fact that **the LHC is really big**!

The LHC works by firing **two beams of particles**, almost always **protons**, at each other. The beams travel in opposite directions in specially constructed **vacuum** tubes, designed so the protons avoid colliding with any other molecules.

The beams inside the LHC collide at **four different points** around the ring, where four particle detectors are located—the **ATLAS, CMS, ALICE,** and **LHCb**. Electromagnetic fields maintained by the superconducting electromagnets guide the beams around the ring at speeds of up to **0.999999991** times the **speed of light**, or approximately **299,792,455** meters per second. This requires cooling the magnets to temperatures of **-456.34°F (-271.3°C)**—colder than outer space.

The most significant discovery made by the Large Hadron Collider was a particle, in **July 2012**, that was later confirmed to be the **Higgs boson**, an elementary particle whose existence was theorized by British physicist **Peter Higgs (1929–)** in 1964. His theory proposed that an **energy field** (the Higgs field) exists **throughout the entire universe**.

As particles move around this field, they **interact** with and **attract** Higgs bosons. The more Higgs bosons a particle attracts, the greater its mass will be. It is essentially a special type of particle that **gives matter its mass** and its discovery is regarded as one of the **greatest breakthroughs in modern science**.

CHAPTER

4

HISTORY

THE SEVEN WONDERS OF THE ANCIENT WORLD

The Seven Wonders of the Ancient World are a selection of **remarkable architectural feats** from antiquity. They are the **Great Pyramid of Giza,** the **Hanging Gardens of Babylon,** the **Temple of Artemis at Ephesus,** the **Statue of Zeus at Olympia,** the **Mausoleum at Halicarnassus,** the **Colossus of Rhodes,** and the **Lighthouse of Alexandria.**

The list of "seven wonders" began as far back as the **1st century** BC, where it originated not as a canon of marvels, but as a kind of **guidebook.** The ancient Greek word for "wonders" is *theumata,* but in the earliest versions of the list, they are described as *theamata,* the ancient Greek word for **"sights."**

Of the Seven Wonders, only one remains **largely intact:** the Great Pyramid of Giza, also known as the **Pyramid of Khufu,** named for its commissioner and posthumous resident. Several of the other remaining wonders exist in various states of ruin:

the sites of the Temple of Artemis and the Mausoleum at Halicarnassus were both **rediscovered in the 19th century,** and the ruins of the Lighthouse of Alexandria were **found underwater in the 20th century**. Though the statues of Zeus and the Colossus of Rhodes have been destroyed, **evidence of their manufacture** has been found in archeological expeditions.

Only the Hanging Gardens of Babylon have **left no physical trace,** with scholars debating whether they actually existed, or were a **creation of poets and writers.** One writer credits the gardens to **King Nebuchadnezzar II,** who built them for a Queen who had grown up in the mountains and missed her home terrain. Some modern scholars posit that the gardens were **not Babylonian** at all, but rather the work of **King Sennacherib of Assyria,** who had aimed to create a **"Wonder for All Peoples."**

MAGELLAN "CIRCUMNAVIGATES" THE WORLD

In the **late 15th and early 16th centuries**, a pressing concern for the Spanish was finding a **new sailing route to Asia**, after the Portuguese had reserved all the routes going east around Africa. Attempting to realize the **original intention of Christopher Columbus (1451–1506)**—a direct route from Europe to the Indies—Magellan proposed an expedition sailing west to Asia to the **Spanish King, Charles I**.

Magellan and his principal scientific advisor **Rui Faleiro** were made captains by Charles and given a fleet of **five ships with a total crew of over 200 men**. They set sail from Seville, Spain, on **August 10, 1519**, paused at the Canary Islands, and then on to Brazil. From there, they made their way down the coast of South America, keeping an eye out for the **fabled passage to the Pacific**.

On **October 21, 1520**, at Cape Virgenes, the fleet **discovered the passage** that would become known as the **Strait of Magellan**. The 373-mile (600-km) passage was arduous to sail through, and only **three of the original five ships** made it to the Pacific Ocean, named by Magellan because of its **apparent calm**. They **reached the Philippines** in March of 1521. There, at Cebu, the chieftain **Rajah Humabon** convinced Magellan to attack **Datu Lapu-Lapu**, an enemy of the Rajah, on the smaller island of Mactan. **Magellan was killed** in the attack, and Lapu-Lapu refused to return the explorer's body.

Of the five original ships, only the *Victoria*, captained by **Juan Sebastián Elcano**, set sail for Spain on December 21, 1521. **Elcano reached Spain** on September 6, 1522, nearly three years after they left. Of the over 200 men who left on the voyage, **only 17 returned with Elcano**.

Ironically, though Magellan is remembered for being the first to circumnavigate the globe, he **neither intended to circumnavigate it** nor did he ever actually **complete the circumnavigation**.

THE BLACK DEATH

One of the **worst pandemics in human history**, the **Black Death ravaged Eurasia** from **1347–52**, killing **75–200 million people** and reducing Europe's overall population by 30–60%. Widely attributed to the bacterium *Yersinia pestis*, the disease was spread by **fleas living on the backs of black rats**, who in turn were transported by **trade ships**, which allowed for **swift transmission** throughout the continent.

The Black Death is thought to have **originated in the grasslands of Central Asia**, where the hosts of *Y. pestis* lived on rodents. The **changing climate** drove these creatures into more populated areas, where they infected local residents.

Traveling either through the **Silk Road** or via **trading ships**, a turning point seems to have been at the city of Kaffa, where a **Mongol army** catapulted **infected corpses** over the city walls during a siege.

The disease arrived first in Europe on the **island of Sicily** in October of 1347, brought by a **fleet of Genoese trading ships** who had been at Kaffa; from there, **outbreaks occurred in Pisa** and **Marseille**. By June 1348, the plague had spread to **France, Spain, Portugal, and England**, and continued across **Germany and Scandinavia** through 1350, arriving in **Russia by 1351**.

The most commonly noted symptoms were lumps that would occur near the groin, neck, or armpits, and would **seep pus and blood** when punctured. From there, infected victims would **vomit blood** and break out in **high fever**, and most would be **dead within a week**.

LECTURE NUMBER

34

THE INDUSTRIAL REVOLUTION

The Industrial Revolution, **from around 1760 to 1830**, refers to the **mechanization of manufacturing and production methods**, replacing limited **hand craftsmanship** for more efficient **machine tools**, and the rise of **factories**.

A **series of new technologies** in concert provided the **rapid growth** that fundamentally changed the world. Innovations in **textile manufacture, steam power, iron production, and the creation of machine tools**, all worked together to **change the landscape of manufacturing**.

In the world of textiles, a **back-and-forth race** between **weaving technology** and **spinning technology** drove innovation. First, advances in weaving technology with **the flying shuttle** had weavers outpacing the thread-spinners. Then, over the course of the 18th century, **thread and yarn production improved dramatically**, requiring more weaving innovation. By the early 19th century, **machine-made cloth**, though of lower quality than hand-woven cloth, was **so cheap** that it collapsed the hand-woven cloth industry.

Similar progress in **iron processing** allowed greater production and versatility. Moving from **wood- to coal-based furnaces**, and then on to **coke furnaces**, produced an iron that was suitable for **buildings and bridges**. This new process also lowered the cost of iron, helping a number of other industries, **especially manufacture of hardware**.

The **steam engine** may be the most important part of the Industrial Revolution, allowing for **captured energy** to be put to **manufacturing use**. Steam engines were used in factories to **power mills and textile machines**; they powered **bellows that heated iron furnaces**, and they would become the first sources of energy for **the burgeoning railways**.

Finally, the **development of tools** and parts created not by hand but by machine allowed for **greater uniformity** and **interchangeability**. As machines became more complicated, it became much cheaper to have parts that could be **easily and precisely replaced**. These developments **reverberated throughout society**, having profound impacts on **culture, politics, economics, trade**, and the machinery of **war**.

THE FIRST MODERN OLYMPICS

Inspired by the **ancient Olympic Games**, which took place between the 8th century BC and the 4th century AD in Olympia, Greece, the **modern Olympic Games** were the brainchild of French historian **Pierre de Coubertin** (1863–1937). Other, smaller-scale **Olympic-style competitions** had occurred in the intervening centuries, including a 17th–century "Cotswold Games" in England, an 18th–century *"L'Olympiade de la République"* in Revolutionary France, and a Swedish manifestation of the games in the mid-19th century.

De Coubertin was particularly inspired by the **Wenlock Olympic Games**, an annual sports festival held in Shropshire, UK, as well as games put on by Greek businessman **Evangelis Zappas**. In 1894, de Coubertin organized a congress at the **Sorbonne**, in Paris, laying out his plans to the representatives of athletics societies from 11 different countries. It was decided that **the first games would be held in Athens** two years later, in **1896**.

After several **crises of leadership and funding**, and amid political turmoil in Greece, the first opening ceremonies of the modern Olympics took place on **April 6, 1896**. Over the next 10 days, **241 athletes from 14 nations** participated in nine different sports: **athletics, cycling, fencing, gymnastics, shooting, swimming, tennis, weightlifting, and wrestling**. Unlike the later tradition of awarding the first, second, and third place winners with gold, silver, and bronze medals, respectively, first place winners were given a **silver medal** and second place winners a **copper medal**, along with a laurel wreath and a diploma. Overall, the **United States led the medal count** at the games, winning 11 medals, with the host country Greece one behind with 10.

The tradition of the modern Olympic Games has **lasted more than a century**, with games being held every four years with the exceptions of **1916, 1940, and 1944**, which were **cancelled during the world wars**.

THE SPARK THAT IGNITED WORLD WAR I

While there's still much debate over the myriad forces that came together to create the tinderbox that would explode into **World War I**, most historians can agree on a pivotal turning point: the **assassination** of Austrian Archduke **Franz Ferdinand** in Serbia.

Tensions between Austria-Hungary and Serbia had been especially high since 1903, when a **military coup in Serbia** removed an **Austria-Hungary-friendly** dynasty for a **much more nationalistic one**. When Austria-Hungary decided to **annex Bosnia and Herzegovina**, the Serbian assassination of Austro-Hungarian officials became a frequent occurrence.

On **June 28, 1914, Ferdinand was sent to Sarajevo** to open a state museum. It was there that a group of assassins, organized by the **secret military society known as the Black Hand**, was sent to assassinate Ferdinand.

The original plan was to bomb the Archduke's car, but the attempt failed. However, one of the assassins, **Gavrilo Princip**, positioned himself where he believed the Archduke's car would pass on its return journey. Due to a series of lucky (or unlucky, depending on your perspective) events, Princip found himself within five feet of his target. He **shot and killed Ferdinand**, and his wife, Sophie.

Diplomatic maneuvers throughout July **attempted to avoid the outbreak of war**, but by late July, **Austria-Hungary and Serbia had declared war on one another**. Over the next two days, **Russia mobilized** in support of Serbia. Germany insisted Russia stand down, Russia refused, and **Germany mobilized and declared war on Russia**. Germany told France to **renounce its alliance** with Russia, but on **August 1 Germany invaded Luxembourg**.

On August 2, the **Germans asked for free passage through Belgium** to get to France, but King Albert refused, and on August 3 and 4, **Germany declared war on France and Belgium**, respectively. This **violated Belgian neutrality**, which in turn led to **Britain declaring war on Germany**, leading to World War I or **The Great War**. A ceasefire was called on **November 11, 1918**–"the eleventh hour of the eleventh day of the eleventh month."

ROSA PARKS

Rosa Parks (1913–2005) was a **civil rights activist** who played a pivotal role in **protesting against racial segregation** in the American South. She is most widely known for **refusing to give up her seat** on a segregated bus in Montgomery, Alabama, an incident which helped spark the famous and effective **Montgomery bus boycott**, often seen as the first major success of the **Civil Rights Movement**.

Parks worked as a seamstress and a housekeeper, but was also involved with the Civil Rights Movement: her husband, Raymond, was a member of the **National Association for the Advancement of Colored People (NAACP)**, and eventually Parks joined as well. She was elected secretary of the Montgomery chapter of the NAACP, joined the **Voters' League**, and attended the **Highlander Folk School**, where racial equality and workers' rights activists were trained.

On December 1, 1955, **Parks boarded a Montgomery City Lines** bus, and sat in the front row of the "colored" section, meant for African Americans. At the time, custom in Montgomery was that if the **"white" section** filled up, the driver would **move back the divider** and the African American passengers would be **asked to move back**.

But in this particular instance, when asked to move, **Parks refused and stayed in her seat**. When the bus driver threatened her with police arrest, she replied, **"You may do that."** Parks was **arrested and booked** on violating the segregation law.

Parks was arrested on a Thursday; that Monday the Montgomery bus boycott began, **involving tens of thousands of black commuters**. They carpooled, took taxis, and walked—ultimately, the **boycott lasted 381 days**. In the end, the city **repealed its segregation law** after it was declared unconstitutional by a separate case, *Browder v. Gayle*. To this day, the story of Parks not giving up her seat is a **cornerstone of the history of the Civil Rights Movement**.

STALINGRAD

Raging from **August 1942 to February 1943**, the **Battle of Stalingrad** was the **largest and bloodiest** battle of World War II, resulting in nearly **2 million people being killed, wounded, or captured**. It was also a **crucial turning point** in the war, described by some as the **biggest defeat** in the history of the German Army.

By 1942, the German expansion to the east had captured Ukraine, Belarus, and the Baltic Republics, and bolstered by these successes, **Hitler redirected** the goals of the 1942 campaign to **include the occupation of Stalingrad** in the southern Soviet Union. Named for the **Soviet leader**, the city took on a highly **symbolic and propagandistic significance** as the war progressed.

The **German 6th Army** reached Stalingrad on **August 23, 1942**, driving Russian forces into the city. The Soviets **moved supplies** like grain and cattle out of the city and **across the Volga river**, but failed to do so for **Stalingrad's citizens**. Some 400,000 civilians remained in the city as the **Germans began their aerial attacks**, dropping 1,000 tons of bombs in the first two days. By February of 1943, only a **tenth of the civilians** of Stalingrad were still living there.

The first **German attempt to take the city** came on September 14, 1943, and the **urban warfare** that ensued was brutal. **Firefights raged** in factories, houses, apartments, and offices; advances weren't block-by-block, they were **door-by-door**, and sometimes, the soldiers joked, **room-by-room**. The costs to both sides were **astronomical**, but the Russians were able to **resupply with personnel from the east**—the Germans were not.

By late November, the **Germans had captured 90% of the city** and had reached the banks of the Volga, but they were **not adequately equipped** to hold their gains. A **series of operations** by the Russians resulted in the Germans being **surrounded and trapped**. Over the next two months the **Germans were slowly starved** of food and ammunition, and by late January, **they were overrun**. On **February 2, 1943**, the Germans **finally surrendered**.

THE BIRTH OF THE INTERNET

Considering how much the Internet has changed the world in the last 30 years, it is still **difficult to pinpoint** its precise origin. **Electronic computers** had been in development since the 1950s, and networking those computers followed naturally. The earliest precursors to the Internet, including the **NPL** (National Physical Laboratory) **network** in the UK, and **ARPANET** (the Advanced Research Projects Agency Network), **developed by the US Department of Defense**, used **packet switching**, which provided more reliable communication.

By 1973, there were several **independent networks** functioning in different parts of the world, and efforts began to **try to unify them**. The first step was to create a **common network language**, known as Transmission Control Program, which would help the disparate networks communicate with one another. **You can still see this skeleton** of the early Internet by opening up the Network settings on your computer, and looking for **"TCP/IP"** which stands for **Transmission Control Protocol and Internet Protocol**. By 1983, TCP/IP was the universal communication protocol.

In the mid-1980s, the **National Science Foundation** in the US created the NSFNET (National Science Foundation Network), meant to connect the different NSF supercomputing centers. When it was **interlinked with ARPANET** in the late 1980s, the term "Internet" came more into use as referring to the **large, global TCP/IP network**.

Meanwhile, beginning in the late 1970s and throughout the 1980s, **networking services for personal computers** began to proliferate, using communication via telephone lines. **CompuServe was the first PC service** in 1979, offering email and creating the first chatrooms.

The final piece of the Internet genesis puzzle was the **creation of the World Wide Web by Tim Berners-Lee** (1955–) in 1989. The web established an **information space** for sharing **documents, sound, video, images, and a multitude of other resources**. Eventually, the Internet and the World Wide Web would **transform culture**, the **economy**, our **social lives**, and, as we've seen most recently, our **political landscape**.

THE FALL OF THE BERLIN WALL

The Berlin Wall, the most potent symbol of the **Cold War divide** between the capitalist West and the communist East, **fell on November 9, 1989**.

The city, which had been **divided since the end of World War II** between its allied conquerors, was split once again, with the French, British, and American sectors in the west, and the Soviet sector in the east. Throughout the **1940s and 1950s**, the USSR increased its grip on its newly acquired **"Eastern Bloc,"** including East Germany, causing many people to **attempt to flee** to the West, especially the **professional class**. Even as the East German government introduced penalties for those trying to emigrate, the **porous border** between East and West Berlin made those efforts **useless**.

Construction of the wall began in 1961; the border was **officially closed on August 13**, and the first of the concrete blocks was installed on August 17. Accompanying the physical barrier were **barbed wire fences and a large "no man's land"** where guards could fire at those attempting to escape. For the next **28 years,** the wall loomed large in the East-West divide. Approximately **5,000 people successfully defected** to West Berlin; the number of those who died trying is disputed, but is thought to be anywhere from 140 to over 200.

Beginning in 1985, the **iron grip of the USSR began to loosen** on the countries of the Eastern Bloc. Following revolutions in **Czechoslovakia and Hungary** in 1989, East Germans began flooding to those countries to **flee to the West**. Finally, it was decided that **border crossings in Berlin** would be opened on **November 10**. However, the East German spokesman who delivered this news on the eve of November 9 had not been fully briefed on the new regulation, and when asked by a reporter when it went into effect, he said, **"As far as I know, it takes effect immediately."**

Crowds swelled at the border crossings, with border guards being uncertain what to do. Finally, due to the sheer numbers, people began to be let through. **West Germans** welcomed their Eastern brethren with **flowers and bottles of Champagne**.

CHAPTER

5

ARTS

MUSIC

& FILM

THE GOLDEN RATIO

The golden ratio is a **ratio between two lengths** that is particularly important in architecture and art for its **visually pleasing quality**. The golden ratio goes back to **Ancient Greek mathematician Euclid** (c. 325–285 BC), who described it in his book ***Elements*** in c. 300 BC, but it was the Italian mathematician **Luca Pacioli** (c. 1447–1517) who helped to popularize it beyond the field of mathematics with his book ***De divina proportione*** in 1509. Pacioli was a friend and collaborator to one **Leonardo da Vinci** (1452–1519), who we'll come back to.

Here's how it goes: first, take a line cut into two different lengths. **The longer portion (a) divided by the smaller portion (b) is equal to the whole line length (a+b) divided by the longer part (a).** It works out as approximately **1: 0.6180339887**, or as a decimal, **1.6180339887**.

The golden ratio is closely linked to the **Fibonacci sequence**—the series of numbers where the next number is found by adding together the two numbers before—0, 1, 1, 2, 3, 5, 8, and so on. If you take any sequential Fibonacci number, for example 5 and 8, and divide the larger number by the smaller, you end up with 1.6. **The larger the Fibonacci numbers, the closer the ratio between them gets to 1.618.** For example, 4181/2584 = 1.6180340557.

So which buildings, paintings, and drawings exhibit the golden ratio in their design? Leonardo da Vinci used the golden ratio to work out key measurements in his painting ***The Last Supper***–for example, the dimensions of the table. He also used it to design his **Vitruvian Man** and the **Mona Lisa**. The **Parthenon** in Greece, the **Great Pyramid** of Giza, **Notre Dame Cathedral**, and the **Taj Mahal** all have lengths and heights approximately equal to the golden ratio. The French composer **Claude Debussy** (1862–1918) even used the golden ratio in the lengths of the bars of *Dialogue du vent et de la mer*.

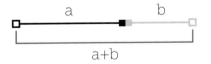

[a+b] is to [a] as [a] is to [b]

THE SISTINE CHAPEL

The Sistine Chapel is located in the **Vatican Palace** in Vatican City, Rome, and serves as the pope's private chapel. It is named after **Pope Sixtus IV**, who was pope from 1471–1484 and who, in 1477–80, oversaw the restoration of a medieval fortified hall known as the **Cappella Magna** into what became the Sistine Chapel. From the exterior, the chapel is a plain, high-sided, rectangular brick building, with no grand entranceway; all passages into the chapel are internal.

The chapel's interior walls feature frescoes depicting major events during the life of Christ, and were painted between 1481–83 by several pre-eminent artists, including **Sandro Botticelli** (c. 1445–1510), who later painted *The Birth of Venus*.

The most famous artworks in the chapel are the ceiling frescoes commissioned by **Pope Julius II**, who was pope from 1503–13, and painted by **Michelangelo Buonarroti** (1475–1564) between 1508 and 1512.

The frescoes feature **nine** scenes from the Book of Genesis, including ***The Creation of Adam***, in which God is depicted almost touching Adam's left index finger, and ***The Fall of Man*** in the Garden of Eden. In a deviation from the story in *The Bible*, Michelangelo depicted a fig rather than an apple, and the serpent is half-serpent, half-woman. A popular myth is that Michelangelo painted the **69-ft (21-m)** high ceiling on his back from a scaffold, but he actually devised a **specialized platform** that enabled him to stand upright to paint it.

Michelangelo was later commissioned to paint the altar wall, a fresco known as ***The Last Judgment***, which he worked on from 1536–41. Some of his more prominent nude male figures in *The Last Judgment* were altered, after the **1564 Council of Trent** condemned nudity in religious art.

The year after Michelangelo's death, artist **Daniele de Volterra** (1509–66) was commissioned to paint underwear on the "indecent" nudes, earning him the nickname **Il Braghettone** (the "breeches maker").

IMPRESSIONISM

Impressionism is the name given to a hugely **influential** 19th-century art movement that attempted to capture the world **as it appeared**, with **spontaneous brushstrokes** conveying the **depth**, **movement**, and **rapidly changing** effect of sunlight in everyday scenes. Impressionism is rooted in the idea of painting **outside** (*en plein air*) in front of the subject rather than relying on sketches in a studio. This approach stood in stark contrast to the classical-themed, academy-sanctioned art that preceded it.

The term "Impressionism" was originally a **derogatory remark** made by French painter and art critic **Louis Leroy** (1812–85) after he had witnessed the first exhibition of what we would now term "impressionist" paintings.

The year was **1874** and a 30-strong group calling themselves the **Anonymous Society of Painters, Sculptors, Engravers etc.** exhibited their work at 35 Boulevard des Capucines in **Paris**. The members included Claude **Monet** (1840–1926), Pierre Auguste **Renoir** (1841–1919), Camille **Pissarro** (1830–1903), Paul **Cézanne** (1839–1906), and Edgar **Degas** (1834–1917).

The very notion of holding an art exhibition outside a dedicated gallery at the time was **radical**, and the paintings themselves would have seemed like **amateurish works in progress** rather than finished articles. Leroy made his disparaging remark in reference to Claude Monet's painting *Impression: Sunrise*, a term the group would later use to describe themselves. **Seven** further exhibitions took place at regular intervals until **1886**.

The Impressionists were influenced by several eminent artists, notably **Gustave Courbet** (1819–77) who focused on ordinary, unidealized scenes, and the expressive brushstrokes of Romantic French painter **Eugène Delacroix** (1798–1863).

The hallmarks of impressionist style are its **vivid colors**, lack of intricate detail, emphasis on **natural light**, and its subject matter of landscapes and scenes of **everyday life**. **The most expensive** Impressionist painting is *Nymphéas en fleur* by Monet, which sold for **$84.6 million** in 2018.

POP ART

Pop art was a movement that began in Britain in the mid-1950s and in the US in the latter part of that decade. Its origins lay in a rejection of fine art in favor of everyday items from **popular culture**, including **advertisements**, **brand designs**, **comic books**, and images of **celebrities**.

American and British pop art can be distinguished by the fact that British exponents viewed US popular culture from **afar**, while the American experience was a **direct reaction** to what they **saw** and **experienced**.

The seeds of pop art were sown in the 1920s, with American modernist painters **Gerald Murphy** (1888–1964), **Charles Demuth** (1883–1935), and **Stuart Davis** (1892–1964) using pop culture imagery in their art.

Marcel Duchamp (1887–1968), the leader of the avant-garde **Dada** movement in the US, also exerted a profound influence on pop art, fusing art with everyday life by **championing mass-production items**, examples of which outraged the art establishment.

Possibly the most significant pop art works were created by **Andy Warhol** (1928–87) and **Roy Lichtenstein** (1923–97). Warhol's ***Campbell's Soup Cans*** comprises **32** identically sized rectangular canvases featuring the varieties of soup produced by the company. The critics were **ruthless**, with the ***Los Angeles Times*** declaring that "This young 'artist' is either a soft-headed fool or a hard-headed charlatan."

The iconic painting ***Whaam!*** was painted in 1963 by Lichtenstein and features a **fighter plane** firing a rocket at a second plane, which explodes dramatically, and a comic book-style "WHAAM!" in big, bright yellow letters. *Whaam!* was inspired by an image in DC Comics' 1962 series ***All American Men of War***. It was bought by the **Tate Gallery** in 1966, a move viewed as controversial both by the art world and the public. But the gamble paid off—**huge crowds** came to see it. Pop art quickly **spread across the world** and still **has an impact** on popular culture today.

LA TRAVIATA

La Traviata ("The fallen woman") is an opera by Italian composer **Giuseppe Verdi** (1813–1901) and tells the tragic love story between **Violetta Valéry**, a courtesan, and her young admirer **Alfredo Germont**.

The opening act is a party hosted by Violetta in her house in **Paris**, where it is revealed that she has been suffering from a **recent illness** (tuberculosis). The **chemistry** between Alfredo and Violetta becomes apparent, but she is soon struck by a **dizzy spell**; soon after, Alfredo confesses he has **loved her from afar** for a year. She tells him **she cannot return his affection**.

The second act fast-forwards three months, where Violetta and Alfredo are living together in a **country house near Paris**. Alfredo learns that she has **sold all her belongings** to fund their new lifestyle. At a friend's party, Violetta is accosted by Alfredo's father **Giorgio**, who insists that she must **end their relationship** because Violetta's reputation **jeopardizes** his daughter's **engagement**. She agrees, earning the respect of Giorgio.

Violetta arrives at her friend's ball with her former lover **Baron Douphol**. Alfredo appears and starts **winning at the gaming tables**. Seeing Violetta and Douphol, Alfredo loudly states that he **will take her home with him**. The Baron is about to challenge Alfredo to a **duel** but is **averted** by Violetta who encourages him to gamble against Alfredo instead. During a break, Violetta urges Alfredo to leave, believing his life to be in danger. He says **he will only leave if she comes with him**. Violetta tells him she is **bound by an oath** to leave him. When Alfredo asks her if she loves the Baron, she answers yes, grief-stricken. Heartbroken, Alfredo **throws his winnings** at her in payment for her services. He is castigated by the other guests and the **Baron challenges him to a duel**.

Violetta tells Alfredo that he can't comprehend the **depth of her love** for him and the **sacrifices** she has made. **The lovers are reunited** in the final scene, but Violetta's consumption has worsened. Giorgio arrives, full of **remorse** for his actions. Violetta **miraculously revives**, proclaiming that her pain has left her and she feels strong again, but then **dies in Alfredo's arms**.

La Traviata is one of the most commonly performed and influential operas, inspiring the movie ***Pretty Woman*** (1990) and Baz Luhrmann's ***Moulin Rouge!*** (2001). It features some of the **most difficult music in the soprano repertoire**.

CITIZEN KANE

Citizen Kane was the first feature film from director, actor, and writer **Orson Welles** (1915–85), which he made aged **25** in **1941**. It is a masterpiece of storytelling, for which Welles jointly won an **Oscar** for **Best Original Screenplay**, and a landmark in technical cinematic achievement, using **nonlinear narrative**, unusual camera angles, and snappy, overlapping dialog.

Citizen Kane begins at **Xanadu**, the palatial residence of **Charles Foster Kane**, a character partly inspired by newspaper magnate **William Randolph Hearst** (1863–1951). Kane is on his deathbed and utters "**Rosebud**" before dropping a **snowglobe** containing a simple snow-covered scene. Kane's death is **front-page news** around the world, and reporter **Jerry Thompson** is tasked with uncovering the meaning of his mysterious final word.

The film tells the story of Kane's life through **flashbacks**. The young Kane's tale begins in **poverty** in Colorado until a **gold mine** is found under his parent's property. Contentedly playing with his **sled** in the **snow**, he is suddenly sent away to be **educated** and groomed for **high society life**. **His mother is supportive of the idea**, partly to take him away from his **violent father**.

Kane inherits a **huge fortune** and business empire on his 25th birthday. He acquires *The New York Daily Inquirer*, which he uses to publish **scandalous, sensationalist** stories and **manipulate public opinion** that drags the US into the **Spanish-American War**. Kane marries the **niece of the President**—a **platform** from which he can launch his **political ambitions**. The relationship falls apart and Kane embarks on an affair with amateur singer **Susan Alexander**. **The snowglobe is visible on a counter when the two meet**.

Kane runs for **Governor of New York**, establishing himself as a **friend of the masses**, a reformer who will clean up corruption. However, his **affair ruins his marriage and political ambitions**. He marries Susan and forces her to become an opera singer. After she leaves him, he is inconsolable, **abandoned by the second woman that he has loved in his life**. He destroys his bedroom until he spots the snowglobe and says "Rosebud."

Back at Xanadu, Kane's belongings are being **burnt in a furnace. Thompson states that he can't solve the mystery of Kane's final word**. The film ends zooming in on the **burning sled** that Kane played on before he was sent away as a child. It bears the name "Rosebud."

Despite the near-unilaterally positive reviews it received upon release, *Citizen Kane* **failed to recoup its costs**, in part down to Hearst's influence **banning it at theaters** and keeping any mention of the film out of his newspapers.

BLUES LEGENDS

Blues music first emerged in the **Mississippi Delta**, Texas, and Appalachia at the beginning of the 20th century. Its strongest influence came in the form of **"spirituals"**—**Christian songs** sung by **slaves** that described their **suffering**. Blues music features unique distinguishing characteristics, such as musical tones that **deviate** from the (do-re-mi) diatonic scale and the involvement of **"blue notes,"** which fall between the intervals of the scale and create a powerful feeling of **melancholy**. Here are profiles of some of the most famous blues musicians:

Howlin' Wolf (1910–76), born Chester Arthur Burnett, was an imposing figure at 6 ft 6 in (2 m) and possessed a deep, powerful, rasping voice that must rank as one of the **most distinctive in any musical genre**. Several of the Chicago blues singer's tracks are legendary and were hugely influential in the development of the blues, most notably "Smokestack Lightnin'" (1956).

Robert Johnson (1911–38) was one of the first blues singer–songwriters to pass into legend. His **unquestionable singing ability, guitar playing, and songwriting skills** gave rise to a popular myth that claimed he sold his soul to the devil at a crossroads in Mississippi to become a famous blues musician. Eric Clapton credits him as "the most important blues singer that ever lived."

Muddy Waters (1913–83) was born McKinley Morganfield and later nicknamed "the father of modern Chicago blues." Although not the first to utilize electric guitar to play the blues—T-Bone Walker (1910–75) was the pioneer—Waters perfected it and influenced not just blues music, but rock, folk, jazz, and country music too. The Rollin' Stones and the popular magazine *Rolling Stone* took their names from his 1950 song "Rollin' Stone."

B.B. King (1925–2015) was a formidable guitar player and prolific performer, playing over 200 gigs a year well into his seventies. **He named his guitars "Lucille"** after the woman that two men fought over at a gig in an Arkansas dance hall in 1949. The story goes that the men knocked over a heater filled with burning kerosene and the hall was evacuated. King ran back inside to fetch his guitar.

Etta James (1938–2012) had a uniquely powerful voice that could instantly shift from gentle to thunderous. She has often been credited as **"bridging the gap between rhythm and blues and rock 'n' roll."** She battled personal problems including heroin addiction and incarceration, channeling her troubles through her music. It was not until the 1990s that her influence and talent were finally rewarded by the establishment with a series of awards.

JAZZ LEGENDS

Originating in African-American communities in New Orleans at the turn of the 20th century, jazz evolved from blues and ragtime into a loosely connected, **hugely influential movement.** Jazz is a constantly shifting style of music, primarily instrumental, with improvisation playing a key part. It has been described as "America's original art form." Here are some of the most famous jazz musicians:

Duke Ellington (1899–1974) was a pianist, composer, and bandleader who began performing professionally at 17, making his name at the **Cotton Club** in Harlem. Over a 50-year career, Ellington elevated jazz to an art form, combining his gift for harmonic invention with an ability to assemble and exploit the talents of the finest orchestral jazz unit ever seen.

Louis Armstrong (1901–71) gained fame in the 1920s for his extraordinary ability and creativity with a trumpet and cornet. As his fame grew, he began to use his **distinctive gravelly voice,** becoming a legend of vocal improvisation. His now-iconic song "We have All The Time in the World" was released in December 1969 but only became a hit 25 years later, after it was used in an advert for Guinness.

Billie Holiday (1915–59) was born Eleanora Fagan and nicknamed "Lady Day" by her saxophonist collaborator Lester Young. She possessed a unique voice and sublime improvisational skills. **Her most influential song** was "Strange Fruit" (1939), based on a poem by Abel Meeropol protesting about African-American lynchings. She first sang it at Café Society in Greenwich Village, New York, the first integrated club in the city. Holiday struggled with narcotics abuse and alcohol addiction, affecting her voice toward the end of her career.

Ella Fitzgerald (1917–96), the "First Lady of Song," was an extraordinary vocalist whose life changed when she won a talent show at New York's Apollo Theater aged 17. She was supposed to dance, but was paralysed by stagefright, unexpectedly singing as the audience became restless. Winner of 14 Grammy awards, she was renowned for perfect diction, a stunning vocal range, and precise timing. Her work with Louis Armstrong produced some of her best-loved music, such as "Cheek to Cheek" and "Dream a Little Dream of Me."

Miles Davis (1926–91) was a renowned trumpet player, composer, and bandleader. He made his debut as a member of legendary musician Charlie Parker's bebop quintet from 1944–8. Davis became an **influential figure** by pushing boundaries, experimenting with new styles and unfamiliar instruments. He was an exponent of modal jazz, which features sparse chords and nonstandard scales instead of chord progressions.

THE BIRTH OF ROCK 'N' ROLL

Rock 'n' Roll is a style of music that emerged in America in the **1950s**, evolving from a diverse range of black musical genres, including **rhythm 'n' blues** and boogie-woogie, and country music.

In the early 1950s, black rhythm 'n' blues vocal groups like **Billy Ward and his Dominoes**, The Clovers, and The Spaniels experimented with a fusion of louder, punchier R&B sounds, raunchier lyrics, and call-and-response arrangements. They piqued the interest of radio DJs, who played their songs, introducing primarily white teenagers to a thrilling, subversive new style of music. A number of adults, outraged by this new style of music, wrote to radio stations denigrating it as "dirty" and calling for censorship.

And then, in July 1954, a shy yet flamboyantly attired 19-year-old by the name of **Elvis Presley** changed everything. His first single "That's All Right" was recorded at **Sun Studio** in **Memphis**; it was completely unplanned—Elvis and his two bandmates had been taking a break and messing around with a cover of bluesman **Arthur Crudup**'s song "That's All Right" of 1946. Producer and founder of Sun Studio **Sam Phillips** heard the session and asked them to record the single. The song sold around **20,000 copies**, enough to ensure regional attention. Within two years, Elvis became an **international phenomenon**, revolutionizing the music world, blurring social lines, and challenging racial barriers.

The answer to the question: what was the first Rock 'n' Roll record? has never been universally agreed upon. **"Rock Around the Clock"** by **Bill Haley & His Comets**, which was released in **May 1955** after originally appearing as a B-side in May 1954, was the first Rock 'n' Roll record to become an **international sensation**, but it wasn't the first Rock 'n' Roll record. The **1949** single **"Rock Awhile"** by the largely forgotten teenager **Goree Carter** makes a good claim, as does **Jackie Brenston's 1951** single **"Rocket 88,"** written by **Ike Turner**, which the **Rock & Roll Hall of Fame** acknowledges is "widely considered the first rock 'n' roll record."

JAWS AND STAR WARS: THE BIRTH OF THE BLOCKBUSTER

Jaws (1975) is regarded as cinema's first **"summer blockbuster."** It became the highest-grossing film of all time, launched **Steven Spielberg**'s career, and made us think twice about what might be lurking beneath even the bath water. Universal spent **$2 million** on a **revolutionary marketing campaign** that included prime-time TV adverts, and the now **iconic movie poster**. The film was released at a time when a **new generation** of moviegoers had time and money to spend. The recent proliferation of **multiplex cinemas** was the perfect commercial answer.

However, the making of the movie was far from plain sailing, running **vastly overbudget** and behind schedule. On the first day of shooting, the **mechanical shark**, named **Bruce** after Spielberg's lawyer Bruce Ramer, sank. Ongoing mechanical issues meant that most scenes were shot without the shark, which doesn't actually appear until **81 minutes** through the film.

However, a film was released two years later that had an even greater cultural impact: *Star Wars*. Originally titled *The Adventures of Luke Starkiller*, it changed the cinematic landscape forever, pioneering the idea of **a movie universe**, launching the **science-fiction genre** on a major commercial level, and associating the term "blockbuster" with a **visual-effects-driven epic**. Part of the genius of *Star Wars* lay in the unexplored parts of the universe, which gave viewers a platform to **imagine their own adventures**, paving the way for **fan-fiction** and establishing a huge appetite for **tie-in merchandise**.

When **20ᵗʰ Century Fox** agreed to finance *Star Wars* in 1973, George Lucas secured a deal that only paid him **$150,000**, but provided him with **the rights to make the sequels**. Lucas also gained control of **all merchandising rights**, establishing complete control over the Star Wars empire. Lucas eventually sold his company, **Lucasfilm**, for **$4.05 billion** to **Disney** in 2012. Actor **Alec Guinness**, who famously described Star Wars as **"fairytale rubbish"** also earned a vast sum of money thanks to his agent, who secured him **2.15%** of the total profits. By the time of his death in 2000, he is thought to have made **$81m** from the film.

INDEX